M is for Maple

A Canadian Alphabet

Written by Mike Ulmer and Illustrated by Melanie Rose

Sleeping Bear Press
310 North Main Street
P.O. Box 20
Chelsea, MI 48118
www.sleepingbearpress.com

Printed and bound in Canada.

10 9 8 7 6 5 4 3 2 1

Library of Congress Cataloging-in-Publication Data
ISBN: 1-58536-051-1

Ulmer, Michael, 1959-
   M is for maple : a Canadian alphabet / written by Michael Ulmer and illustrated by
Melanie Rose.
      p. cm.
   Summary: Each letter of the alphabet is represented by a name or word derived from
some aspect of the country of Canada, and each term is presented in a rhyme and then
further explained in a note.

1. Canada—Juvenile literature. 2. English language—Alphabet—Juvenile literature.
[1.Canada. 2. Alphabet.] I. Rose, Melanie, ill. II. Title.

F1008.2 .U46 2001
971-dc21   2001032071

That's Canada to me

*From Atlantic to Pacific, from St. John's to B.C.,
there's a place that's like no other, that's Canada to me.*

*We are new maples growing tall, our roots cross time and seas,
to countries all the world around, that's Canada to me.*

*We weren't the first to walk this land, it's written in history
that Natives helped newcomers live, that's Canada to me.*

*Our flag is red, then white, then red, we all take pride to see
different colors standing side by side, that's Canada to me.*

*We all feel the winter's frosty bite and summer's welcome breeze.
We love the land, canoes and camps, that's Canada to me.*

*So meet me where the Mounties ride and lighthouses line the sea.
Where hockey's king, and kindness lives, that's Canada to me.*

To Gracie, the family's newest rhymer.

MIKE ULMER

*My thanks to my parents for inspiring me with
their love of nature and the visual world.*

*To my husband, Darryl, for all his
support and encouragement.*

*To Heather Hughes, Jan Napier and Sleeping
Bear Press for giving me this opportunity.*

MELANIE ROSE

A is for Anne—that's Anne with an E—
a red-headed orphan who loved Avonlea.
The Cuthberts had thought they were adopting a boy,
but that red-headed girl would be their pride and their joy.

Anne of Green Gables is Canada's most famous book. Written by Lucy Maud Montgomery in 1908, it tells the story of an orphan girl, Anne, who is adopted by Matthew and Marilla Cuthbert. The Cuthberts wanted a boy to help with their chores. Instead they got a wonderful little girl who quickly won their hearts.

Before Frederick Banting (*pictured at right*) and Charles Best joined to invent insulin, diabetes was considered a fatal disease. The two men, along with a team of researchers, made their breakthrough in 1922 at the University of Toronto. Their discovery has helped save hundreds of thousands of lives.

"B" also stands for Roberta Bondar, a scientist who gained great fame in 1992 as the first Canadian woman to fly in space. She has a planetarium named after her in Toronto. The first Canadian astronaut to travel in space was Marc Garneau who flew in the American space shuttle *Challenger* in 1984.

Bb

B is for Banting, B is for Best,
true Canadian heroes whose medical quest
gave the world insulin, a new lifesaving way
to keep the effects of diabetes at bay.

C

C is for Canada where it once was a must
that only a male held a position of trust.
      But then came Kim Campbell who knew and believed
that nothing else mattered but the courage to lead.

Kim Campbell was a lawyer and Vancouver school board official first elected to fill a federal seat in 1988. She took over for retiring Prime Minister Brian Mulroney to become our first female prime minister in 1993.

The Dionne Quints were born in May of 1934 in Corbeil, Ontario to Oliva and Elzire Dionne. It was only the third recorded case of quintuplets (or, five babies) in the world. For nine years, the girls lived in a theme park where visitors paid to see them. For this, the provincial government apologized in 1998.

D
d

D means Dionne and five little girls
who drew millions of people from all 'round the world.
Emilie, Cecile, Yvonne made for three.
The set was completed with Annette and Marie.

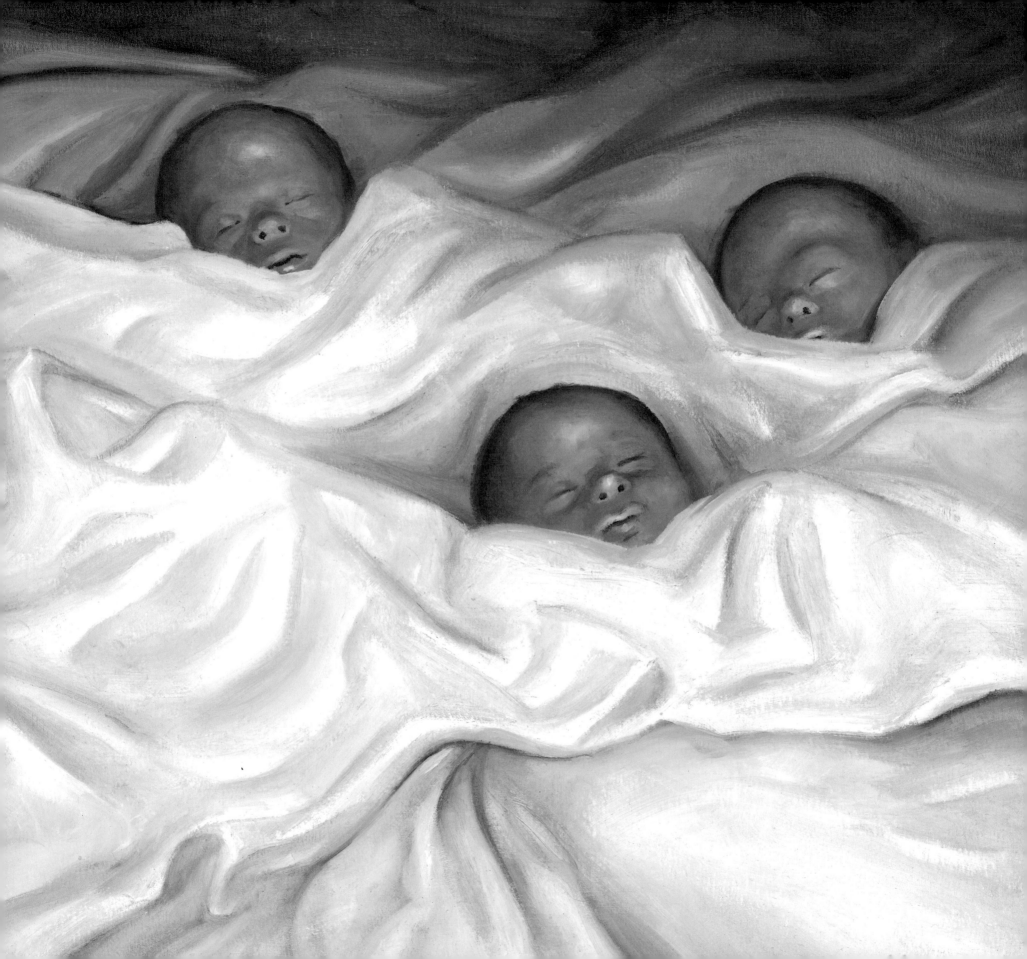

ARCTIC OCEAN
OCEAN ARCTIQUE

ALASKA
(U.S.A.)

GULF OF ALASKA
GULFE D'ALASKA

YUKON
TERRITORY
TERRITOIRE DU
YUKON

GREAT
BEAR LAKE

NORTHWEST TERRITORIES
TERRITOIRES DU NORD-OUEST

NUNAVUT

GREAT SLAVE L.

BRITISH COLUMBIA
COLUMBIE-BRITANNIQUE

L. ATHABASCA

HUDSON

C

A

ALBERTA

N

A

SASKATCHEWAN

MANITOBA

L. WINNIPEG

ONTARIO

PACIFIC OCEAN
OCÉAN PACIFIQUE

UNITED STATES OF AMERICA

LAKE SUPE

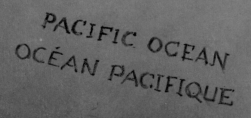

E is for "Eh," our national obsession
for ending each sentence, not with a period, but a question.
It's a Canadian habit, as polite as you please,
to give every listener the chance to agree.

ICELAND

GREENLAND
(DENMARK)

BAFFIN BAY
BAIE DE BAFFIN

DÉTROIT DAVIS STRAIT

LABRADOR SEA
MER DU LABRADOR

D

A

QUÉBEC

LABRADOR

NEWFOUNDLAND
TERRE-NEUVE

NEW
BRUNSWICK
NOUVEAU
BRUNSWICK

P.E.I.

NOVA SCOTIA
NOUVELLE-ÉCOSSE

ATLANTIC OCEAN
OCÉAN ATLANTIQUE

L. HURON

L. ONTARIO

LAKE ERIE

E^e

E also stands for Edmonton, the capital
city of Alberta. Edmonton is known
as the "Gateway of the North" and is
home to the world's largest shopping
centre, the West Edmonton Mall. The
mall has the world's largest indoor
amusement park, Galaxyland, as well
as attractions ranging from a water
park to an ice palace.

Fis a man who in one summer proved
he could do with one leg what few could manage with two.
Terry Fox never finished his cancer crusade;
now we all do the running, and we honour his name.

Ff

Many consider Terry Fox to be the greatest Canadian ever. Terry was 18 when he lost his right leg to cancer. Saddened by the difficulties cancer patients endured, Fox created his Marathon of Hope to raise money for cancer research. He dipped his artificial leg in the Atlantic Ocean in St. John's in April 1980 and began his run across the country. Terry averaged 43 kilometres a day for 143 days and ran over 6,000 kilometres in total. But his cancer returned and he had to end his run in Thunder Bay on September 1, 1980. He died in June, 1981. Terry Fox reached his goal of generating one dollar for every Canadian for cancer research. Over 5,600 Terry Fox Runs are held every year.

Canadian farmers are considered among the world's best. Two-thirds of the grain produced in Canada is exported to any one of 100 countries around the globe.

"G" also stands for Governor General. The Governor General represents the English monarchy and to our most deserving citizens presents the Order of Canada.

G

g

G stands for Grain and the valleys of wheat
    that ripple through the prairies in the dry, summer heat.
Our western-grown bounty is a gift to the globe,
    for the bread of the world comes from seed that we've sown.

H h

About two-thirds of NHL players are born in Canada, and the game is played by boys and girls in rinks and on roads all over the country. Wayne Gretzky, Geraldine Heaney, Mario Lemieux, Gordie Howe, and Hayley Wickenheiser are among the greatest hockey players Canada has produced. England's Governor General to Canada, Lord Stanley, liked the game and paid $50 for a trophy that would be awarded to Canada's best team each year. It was called the Stanley Cup.

H is for Hockey, the game that we play
from summer's last whisper to snow's melting away.
We may never grow to be NHL stars
but it's something we care for; it'll always be ours.

Canada is home to the Thousand Islands region in Ontario (for which Thousand Island salad dressing was named), Salt Spring Islands in British Columbia and countless more. Charlottetown, the capital city of Prince Edward Island, is known as the birthplace of Confederation.

"I" also stands for Iqaluit, which means "place where the fish are." Iqaluit is the capital of Canada's newest territory, Nunavut. About 27,000 people, most of Innu descent, live in Nunavut. Canada's biggest island, Baffin Island, is in Nunavut.

I i

I is for Islands, with no borders of land,
like Montreal, Vancouver and of course, Newfoundland.
In Victoria, in Baffin, and so many more,
you'll find the roar of the water by the quiet of the shore.

J j

J is for Justice, brought by horse to the west
by the Mounted Police in their fiery red vests.
They are known as the Mounties, and they're respected worldwide
for the depths of their courage and their Musical Ride.

The Royal Canadian Mounted Police (RCMP) have been known as "Red Coats" and "Riders of the Plains." They were formed in 1873 to bring order to the West and began with a force of 275 men. The RCMP now employs more than 14,000 men and women. The Mounties Musical Ride, a daring display of equestrian precision, has thrilled audiences all over the country.

K is for Klondike and the hunger for gold
that drew thousands of miners to the northerly cold.
The men made the journey by mule, foot, and teams
to pan for their fortunes in the cold running streams.

In August of 1896, three prospectors discovered gold on Rabbit Creek where the Klondike and Yukon rivers meet. A year later, news hit the American West and the Klondike Gold Rush was on. In all, as many as 100,000 prospectors and people looking for work were said to have rushed to the Klondike. Towns were built almost overnight and doctors charged $200 for each visit. Gold fever gripped the North for two years until the area was tapped out and many miners headed for a new find in Nome, Alaska. People still pan for gold in the Klondike, and in many areas, they keep what they find.

k

K

L is for Louisbourg and the garrison that stands
as evidence of France colonizing this land.
Royal Navy cannons dealt a final defeat;
you can still hear their echo in the shops and the street.

L l

Louisbourg, on what is now New Brunswick's Cape Breton Island, was founded as a French colony in 1713. By 1740, its military value was so appreciated that France surrounded the town with stone walls and cannons. But shelling and a blockade in 1745 by troops from New England and Britain ended French control. France recovered Louisbourg in a treaty but the Royal Army and Navy recaptured it for the final time in 1758.

Long before the first Europeans arrived, Canada's aboriginal peoples had discovered the food properties of maple sap, which they gathered each spring. Historians believe the maple leaf began to serve as a Canadian symbol as early as 1700. In 1957, the colour of the maple leaves on the Coat of Arms of Canada was changed from green to red. On February 15, 1965, the red maple leaf flag was inaugurated as the National Flag of Canada.

"M" also stands for Montreal, which for 150 years stood as Canada's largest city. Montreal is one of the most beautiful cities in the world. Its many attractions include the Biodome, the cobblestoned streets of old Montreal, and, it is said, the country's best bagels.

M is for Maple, our national leaf,
and the Sugar and the Silver that thrive in the East.
The Big Leaf and Douglas prefer west of the plains,
the Manitoba Maple bears its home in its name.

m

M

N is for Northern, the great Northern Lights,
   those mystery visions that light up our nights.
The Innu believed that the lights showed a game
   being played by the Sky People in their heavenly domain.

The scientific name for the Northern Lights is *aurora borealis*, which in Latin means Northern Dawn. The Northern Lights often include vivid combinations of purple, blue, gold and red. On some nights, the lights are as bright as the moon.

"N" also stands for Northern Dancer, one of the greatest thoroughbred racehorses ever. Born in Oshawa, Ontario in 1961, Northern Dancer was the first Canadian horse to win the Kentucky Derby. For a horse, Northern Dancer lived a long life. He died at the age of 29 in 1990. Even today, many of the finest horses can trace their heritage to the great Northern Dancer.

O is Ojibwa,
    just one of the tribes
that spanned this vast country
    before settlers arrived.
    We're Canadians all,
        but we must never forget
        that our land was their land
        and we owe them a debt.

As many as 500,000 aboriginal people were already living in Canada when European settlers arrived in the 16th century. Today, aboriginal people make up three percent of our population, and they include Inuit, Metis and First Nation peoples.

"O" also stands for Ottawa, the capital of Canada. Visitors to Ottawa can see the beautiful Peace Tower and visit its famous winter carnival, Winterlude. Ottawa is also home to the Rideau Canal, the world's longest outdoor skating rink.

Oo

Pis for Peterson and in jazz or in swing,
he is musical royalty, the piano's grand king.
He played with the greatest on stages world 'round,
yet no one could copy his magical sound.

Pp

Oscar Peterson is one of the greatest jazz pianists ever. A Montreal native, he has played with the giants of jazz music including Louis Armstrong and Ella Fitzgerald.

"P" also stands for Peggy's Cove, a famous and beautiful Nova Scotia town. Peggy's Cove is said to have derived its name from a legend. A woman named Margaret survived a shipwreck and was pulled from the bay by villagers. They dubbed the water Peggy's (short for Margaret's) Cove.

Qq

Quebec is where I always go
to ski in "neige"—
that's French for snow,
and "seul" means that
you're by yourself
to lick 'creme glacée'
before it melts.
Oh pity the countries
who must make do
with just one language
instead of two.

Since 1534, when explorer Jacques Cartier declared Quebec the property of France, this province has existed as a unique and wonderful French culture. Quebec stands as Canada's largest province and is bigger than France, Germany, and Spain, combined. Among provinces, only Ontario has more inhabitants than Quebec, which is home to 7.3 million people. Slightly more than 80 percent of Quebec residents list French as their first language.

Many people consider the late Maurice, "Rocket" Richard, the most exciting hockey player ever. A member of the Montreal Canadiens from 1942 to 1960, he was the first NHL player to score 50 goals. He had a very bad temper, and when he was suspended for hitting an official, his fans rioted in downtown Montreal and caused millions of dollars in damage. Maurice's brother Henri was also a great star, but he stood three inches shorter than his brother. Henri was called the "Pocket Rocket."

R is for Rocket—that's Rocket Richard—
A Canadiens' superstar with a shot true and hard.
The sight of no player will ever compare
to those fiery brown eyes and that flying black hair.

S means Stampede and Calgary's the place
to see cowpokes and horses and the chuckwagon race.
The world's greatest rodeo is held each July,
and includes a fine carousel with slower horses to ride.

The Greatest Outdoor Show on Earth, the Calgary Stampede has been a rodeo event since 1912.

"S" also stands for Saint John, New Brunswick's largest city, and St. John's, the capital and largest city in Newfoundland. Sarnia, a city in Southwestern Ontario is my hometown and sells great French fries under the Bluewater Bridge. What letter does your hometown start with? What do you like most about where you live?

S s

t T T

T means Toronto, a place where they say
you can spend a year doing something different each day.
Rides at Ontario Place, see the Blue Jays or Leafs,
explore Casa Loma or Centre Island beach.

Toronto has become Canada's gateway.
Half of Canada's new immigrants settle
in or around Toronto.

"T" also stands for Pierre Trudeau,
one of Canada's most famous prime
ministers. Prime Minister Trudeau,
who wore a fresh red rose on his
jacket every day, died in 2000 in
Montreal. He is best remembered for
the creation of the Canadian Charter
of Rights and Freedoms, which spell
out the privileges of every Canadian.

U speaks to a time when there once was a need
to shelter human beings from the slave owner's greed.
The Underground Railroad helped American slaves
find in Canada the safety and freedom they craved.

Between 1840 and 1860, as many as 30,000 slaves may have crossed into Canada from the United States through a network of safehouses and contacts. Slavery had existed in Canada but was abolished in 1834.

"U" also stands for Ukrainians, immigrants who helped build the West. Fifteen percent of the people who live in Winnipeg, Edmonton, and Saskatoon have a Ukrainian background. The largest group of Ukrainian immigrants arrived between 1896-1914.

U u

V
v

"Victoria" in Canada is the most common name
for cities and roads all named in her reign.
Parks and great mountains and the capital of B.C.
are lasting reminders of this long-ago queen.

From west to east, our provincial
and territorial capitals are: Victoria
(British Columbia), Whitehorse (Yukon),
Yellowknife (Northwest Territories),
Edmonton (Alberta), Regina
(Saskatchewan), Winnipeg (Manitoba),
Toronto (Ontario), Iqaluit (Nunavut),
Quebec City (Quebec), Fredericton
(New Brunswick), Charlottetown
(Prince Edward Island), Halifax (Nova
Scotia) and St. John's (Newfoundland).

There are 70 names for wind in Canada including Dust Devils and Alberta Clippers.

"W" also stands for Winnipeg, the capital city of Manitoba. Portage and Main streets, in downtown Winnipeg, is said to be the coldest corner in Canada, but Winnipeg is far from Canada's snowiest city. Winnipeg's average snowfall is just a third of that of Charlottetown, Prince Edward Island. If you want to stand in the middle of Canada, head to Winnipeg, the closest major city to the exact centre of Canada.

W is for Wind, like the Black Blizzard that blows
unwelcome on the prairies for bringing dirt, not snow.
There are Break-up winds, Chinooks, and more Westerly beasts,
the Wreckhouses are named for what they do in the East.

X marked the spot where the Last Spike was driven;
it was done with a hammer, not the cut of a ribbon.
And with the Last Spike we could finally proclaim
that we were a nation united by train.

Without the railway, there would be no Canada. The completion of the Canadian Pacific Railway was a condition for British Columbia's entry into Confederation. With poor roads and water lines clogged with ice for as many as five months a year, there were no means to deliver people and goods from one end of the country to the other. Canadian Pacific Railway official Donald Smith drove in the final spike on his second try, November 7, 1885, at Craigellachie, in Eagle Pass, British Columbia.

Y y

Y is for Yoho, one of 39 sites
with fast running rivers and dizzying heights.
Our national parks belong to all who would hear
the splash of the salmon and the rustle of deer.

Yoho National Park, 25 kilometres east of Golden, British Columbia, was designated in 1886 and stands among Canada's oldest recognized parklands. We have 39 national parks, from the Pacific Rim National Park in the west to the Gros Morne and Terra Nova National Parks in Newfoundland. More National Parks are being planned, and conservationists are hopeful that when finished, three percent of our land will be devoted to national parks.

The zipper was originally invented by an American, but it was perfected and patented by Canadian Gideon Sundback in 1913. Mr. Sundback would later become president of the Lightning Fastener Company of St. Catharines, Ontario.

Z stands for Zipper, which everyone knows
is very important in tents and in clothes.
A U.S. inventor had a zipperish notion,
but it took a Canadian to get the zipper in motion.

Mike Ulmer

When he isn't writing a sports column for the *Toronto Sun*, Mike Ulmer practices his rhyming skills on his daughters Sadie, Hannah, and Madalyn. He lives in Hamilton, Ontario with his wife Agnes Bongers and also shares space with the family cats, Whisky and Jack.

Melanie Rose

Melanie Rose was born in England, and immigrated to Canada with her family as a child. She designed the poster for the 1992 Toronto International Film Festival, and as a runner (she ran the 1998 New York City Marathon), illustrating the letter "F" affected her deeply. A graduate of the Ontario College of Art, she lives in Toronto with her husband, Darryl.